Tulips

LIZ DOBBS
CONSULTANT CEES BREED

Photographs by Clay Perry

Quadrille

First published in 2007 by
Quadrille Publishing Limited
Alhambra House,
27-31 Charing Cross Road,
London WC2H 0LS

Editorial Director: Jane O'Shea
Creative Director: Helen Lewis
Editor: Laura Herring
Designer: Nicky Collings
Photography: Clay Perry
Consultant: Cees Breed
Production: Denise Stone

Based on material originally published in *Tulip*
This page: Monte Carlo

British Library Cataloguing-in-Publication Data
A catalogue record for this book is available
from the British Library.

ISBN: 978 184400 284 9

Printed in China

Tulips

Contents

Introduction

Delve into the history of the tulip and it seems we have always been mad about them. Even before the Dutch experienced the height of their 'tulipomania' from 1634 to 1637, sultans in the Turkish Empire were ordering their subjects to collect thousands of tulip bulbs with which to fill their pleasure gardens. The tulip's history is also the story of many individuals from all cultures and eras who became obsessed with its beauty.

Tulip have inspired men to do great things – write poetry, plant beautiful gardens, devote a lifetime to breeding the flower – but they have also brought out their darker side. In their quest to possess the tulip, collectors bickered, stole, gambled and squandered fortunes, no doubt leaving a trail of misery behind. For some, the goal was to plant *en masse*, to impress people with their great wealth. For others, the desire to possess or create a particular colour or shape in the flower was paramount, and their activities were secret: even one bulb was enough so long as it was the only one and they owned it.

Today, we are still susceptible to the charms of this superb flower. In spring, regardless of whatever we are already enjoying in our own gardens, we will be making lists of 'must-have' varieties for next year. In a very small way, we are simply following in the footsteps of the great and the good who have gone before – like Sultan Selim II, who ordered 50,000 tulip bulbs for his garden in Constantinople.

The majority of the tulips we grow today are loud, big and beefy compared to the delicate wild species, so how was this dramatic transformation realized?

left: Bred in the 1950s, 'Cape Cod' has unique colourings. Like all Greigii tulips, it has attractive mottled foliage and a neat habit.

Origin of the species

Most wild tulips originated in areas of Central Asia, with the richest source of species being between the Tein-Shan and Pamir Alai mountain ranges, near Islamabad, now the capital of Pakistan. Tulips can also be found growing wild in some parts of Europe such as the Balkans, Spain, Portugal, Italy and Crete, but it is thought that these must originally have been brought over by merchants and travellers coming from Central Asia and that they then escaped into the wild.

We tend to think that the original tulips came from Turkey, but they were also found in Russia, near the Black Sea and in the Crimea – areas that once belonged to the Turkish or Ottoman Empire. In the mid-sixteenth century European travellers brought back tales of brilliant red lilies that were held in high esteem by the Turks.

These are thought to have been tulips. The name tulip is said to have come from the Turkish *tuliban*, or turban – men often tucked a tulip in their turban. The first known report of a tulip growing in a western European garden was made by Conrad Gesner, a botanist who in 1559 saw tulips in a garden owned by Councillor Johannis Heinrich Herwart of Augsburg, Bavaria. The sight and scent impressed him so much that he described them in great detail in a book (*Caspari Collino Pharmocopoeo*) published two years later. He also added that the tulips had come from seed from Constantinople.

right: *Tulilpa fosteriana* tulips were imported to Holland from Central America from 1906. This one, 'Red Emperor', is the best known and was widely used in tulip breeding.

Turkish tulipomania

By this time the Turks were already great admirers of the tulip and in fact had been since as far back as the thirteenth century, when poets had waxed lyrical about the beauty of the flower. The Turkish word for tulip is *lale*, which uses the same letters as Allah, so the flowers were often used a religious symbol. Sultans built palaces with gardens filled with their favourite flowers, which included tulips, and as the Ottoman Empire expanded, so did the style of garden. By the sixteenth century the tulip had become a symbol of the Ottoman Empire, embroidered on robes and painted on to tiles and ceramics.

By the 1630s, there were already reports of many tulips being grown in gardens and offered for sale in shops. The Turks had started, as is human nature, to organize and select the best ones, and to make official lists and rules as to what constituted a perfect bloom. They favoured narrow, pointed petals rather than the fuller, cup-shaped flowers preferred in the West. Nevertheless, there was a two-way traffic in tulips, and by the time of the Tulip Era (*Lale Devri*) of 1703–1730, Sultan Ahmed III was importing vast numbers of bulbs from Holland for his gardens and for tulip festivals. Descriptions of these festivals make them sound almost decadent, and the sultan's subjects were aghast at the cost. Still more poems were penned and an illustrated book that showed 49 tulips was produced around 1725. However, when Ahmed died in 1730, the impetus for tulip worship appeared to die with him.

left: *Tulipa batalinii* is a species of tulip that flowers in mid-spring.

Dutch tulipomania

Among the first tulips to flower in Holland were those planted in August 1593 in a small garden at the University of Leiden by the head botanist, Carolus Clusius. These bulbs would have been a select collection: by this time Clusius was 67 years old, had travelled widely and had built up a network of contacts with whom he exchanged bulbs. The bulbs must have been impressive when they bloomed the following spring, because several people were interested in buying them, but Clusius refused all offers. Not surprisingly, the bulbs were stolen in the dead of night, seed from them was sown, and over a period of years, stocks were gradually built up and distributed.

Once the tulip had a foothold in western Europe it spread rapidly: botanists and merchants swapped bulbs and the wealthy sought them as status symbols. Already they were losing their more modest look,

right: 'Heart's Delight' has flowers that open flat and wide in the sun like a waterlily – a characteristic shared by all *Tulipa kaufmanniana* species tulips.

taking on a showy appearance. Their transformation can be charted in paintings of the time.

As early as the late 1620s, a nursery bulb trade had been established around the town of Haarlem, where the soil was ideal for tulips. Dry bulbs travel well, so it didn't take long before an export business had also been set up, and alongside it, illustrated books were produced to show potential customers what the tulips would look like. At the same time, Amsterdam was thriving as a port and trading centre, and it was a logical extension of this growth to create an exchange there to handle different currencies.

All the ingredients were now in place for bulb trading to begin; add to these the tulip's unpredictable capacity to break into streaks of colour that would result in highly sought-after bulbs, and it is easy to see how, once increasing numbers of people started trading, a sort of madness took over. The price of the bulb depended on its name and form but also, from 1636 onwards, the most sought-after bulbs were sold by weight (measured in *azen*) and these were traded in a tulips futures market. White tulips with breaks of red or purple were the most highly prized – examples of the day included 'Semper Augustus' and 'Viceroy' – and the fact that such broken tulips were less vigorous and harder to increase only added to their desirability.

With more and more people dealing, a crash was inevitable and it came suddenly, early in 1637. While speculators forsook the tulip, those who loved the flower for what it was carried on buying it and growing it in their gardens.

left: The deep canary petals of 'Yellow Empress' will give life to any border.

The French connection

Tulips were also raised in France and what was then Flanders, where many interesting varieties were bred, but the growers there were not as commercially minded as the Dutch. One highly sought-after Flemish variety was 'Louis XVI', a white tulip with purple markings raised by an amateur grower in 1776. 'Mon Trésor' (1875) and 'La Reine' (1860) are two early-flowering French varieties, 30–35cm (12–14in) high, that were once widely used for growing in pots. They are now nearly extinct, but 'Mon Trésor' has been specially photographed for this book (see right) from a private collection in Holland. Meanwhile in England, during the Victorian times, tulips were also often grown in containers and their virtues were extolled by John Mollison in his book *The New Practical Window Gardener*, published in 1879.

right: 'Mon Trésor' was once popular for growing in pots and is now only found in private collections.

The English tulip legacy

The tulips infected with virus that caused tulipomania are sadly no longer sold commercially, but their descendants live on in some private collections. One group that has been very well documented is the English Florist tulips.

At first, English enthusiasts copied the seventeenth-century craze for broken tulips and for a time they were fashionable and a statement of wealth. However, by the early eighteenth century the chattering classes were ridiculing tulips, and the flower found more loyal champions among northern working-class artisans. These people were referred to as 'florists', meaning that they concentrated on a particular flower and made a hobby of breeding and showing it. With home-based employment like weaving or shoemaking they were around during the day, able to tend their flowers. They treasured the tulips and many societies were set up in 1750–1850 to grow and show English Florist tulips. In addition, countries with Huguenot refugees, such as Ireland and Scotland, also invariably started up tulip societies.

The English florists bred their own tulips starting with stock from France and Flanders, and later added in their own seedlings. The first thing that they had to do was obtain a self-coloured tulip of the right shape – a half-sphere. This was called a 'breeder'. After having grown stocks of the breeder for many years, the hope was that it would break into a pattern of streaks and flecks.

Different patterns and colours had their own names: Bizarre meant the bloom was yellow with a pattern of any colour; Byloemen was a white tulip with stripes of

left: At first 'Whittallii' blooms are cup-shaped, then open up into a star.

black or purple; Rose was a white bloom with red or pink markings. There were even terms for the pattern of the markings, which are still used today: 'feathered' describes colour shading in from the edge of the petals, while a 'flame' is the markings that run from the top of the petals towards the base.

To show off their hobby, florists' feasts were regularly arranged in pubs. A meal and a competitive show of tulips would take place with the blooms displayed in brown beer bottles. However, by the 1870s the tulip had started to decline as a florists' flower – more people were working in factories than at home, much of the land where the tulips were grown had been built on, and plants that took less time to cultivate became more popular for showing.

Today, only one of these societies remains, the Wakefield and North of England Tulip Society. It was founded in 1836 and is still active, thanks to the tireless efforts of the Akers family who have been involved for generations. The society even has its own varieties, like the red-and-white 'Wakefield', that are passed down and preserved. There is still a show in Wakefield in May each year at which the tulips are displayed.

A prize-winning tulip needs to have six even petals with clear markings that are similar on each petal. The tulips are grown under shade netting in order to keep them in good condition and they are picked a day or two before the show. English Florist tulips are not actually commercially available, but members of the society often swap surplus bulbs in autumn.

right: 'Oratorio', a little tulip with beautiful mottled leaves and rosy-red blooms.

Tulips today

Thanks to the Dutch, we now have thousands of varieties of tulip and they continue to be the main breeders, growers and exporters of both the bulbs and the cut flowers.

The bulb-growing regions of the Netherlands, or *bollenstreek*, are on the west coast of Holland, centred around Lisse, between Haarlem and Leiden. The famous Keukenhof Garden, a shop window for the bulb industry, was established here in 1949 on what were once sand dunes and beech woods. This was an enterprising move, especially as it was created just four years after the 'hunger winter' following the Second World War, when many Dutch starved to death. At that time, many people walked from the cities to the fields to eat the bulbs. Boiled, they were said to taste sweet, a point noted by Carolus Clusius centuries before.

This isn't recommended as tulips are now listed as being poisonous if eaten. Today, tulips thrive on the free-draining soil at Keukenhof and displays and planting ideas attract around 800,000 visitors a year.

As a guide to the scale of the industry, the Netherlands grow more than three billion tulip bulbs each year, of which they export two billion: one billion to the USA and a further billion to countries including Japan, Germany and the UK. There is commercial tulip bulb growing in England on a modest scale, centred around Spalding in Lincolnshire, where the silty soil of the Fens is ideal. Tulips are also grown in Ireland, Denmark, and Japan – in between rice harvests – as well as in Washington State's Skagit Valley, the Dandenong mountains of Australia, Tasmania and New Zealand's South Island.

left: *Tulipa turkestanica* has uncharacteristic features for a tulip: lots of small flowers per stem that open into a star shape.

Tulip breeding

Growing tulips as cut flowers (by 'forcing' them to flower at set times) is more profitable than producing dry bulbs, so this dictates which varieties are widely available. Half the Dutch-grown cut-flower tulips are made up of just ten varieties, and most breeding is concentrated on the Triumph tulips as these respond well to forcing under glass. It is therefore important for gardeners to redress this balance and choose varieties that are gardenworthy rather than merely easy for forcing.

Tulip breeding takes time. Only one in a thousand seedlings will have worthwhile characteristics, and it can take five to seven years for a seed to produce a flower. Bulking up enough stock to sell could take another 13–15 years. Because the bulbs are clones of the original, once stocks are available you can be sure of what you are getting. In time the vigour of these clones can decline; this may take 40 years or so, but it depends very much on the cultivar.

The tulips in this book belong to Cees Breed's private collection and have been chosen because they are among the best of their type. Many of the firms who bred them are no longer trading as there are now fewer but larger firms.

To create new tulip cultivars, a breeder can cross two plants, collect the seed, raise the offspring and select those with interesting features. But many varieties – the Parrot tulips, for example – have arisen naturally from a mutation, known as a 'sport'. Sports often produce further sports, so you can end up with tulips with similar heights and flowering times but with a range of colours or markings.

left: A Single Early tulip, the warm hues of 'Flair' bring welcome colour in early spring.

Trials and awards

In the UK, the Royal Horticultural Society (RHS) has a Daffodil and Tulip Committee that presents awards to tulips for their garden performance. The selections are based on growing trials, visits to private collections and discussions between experts. The highest award is the Award of Garden Merit (AGM), which is given to plants that are gardenworthy and reasonably easy to grow. The AGM was re-instituted in 1992.

In Holland, the awards are organized by the Tulip Committee of the Royal General Bulb Growers' Association (KAVB). The Trial Garden Award (TGA) is worth looking out for, as it highlights varieties that will perform well in the garden. Other awards that are presented include the Award of Merit (AM), the Early Forcing Award (EFA) and the First-Class Certificate (FCC).

Awards are useful when selecting tulips for planting in the garden. They are a more impartial guide than bulb catalogues and point you towards gardenworthy cultivars, not just those that are good as cut flowers. However, do not be too influenced by awards: your criteria may be different, or you might like a style of tulip that has not been assessed for many years. Visit gardens, particularly in your locality, and note varieties that look good after rain or a hot spell and whose colour and form appeal to you. Try a few of them out and record when and how deeply you planted them, and what their display was like in the following spring.

right: 'Bright Gem', one of the smaller of the Species tulips.

Classification checklist

Pick up any tulip bulb catalogue and you will find the tulips grouped under headings like 'Single Early' and 'Double Late'. This is not done on the whim of the supplier, but is an internationally agreed classification organized by the KAVB (see page 26). Its main purpose is to help people navigate their way around the 2,600 varieties available today.

Broadly speaking the classification is based on flowering season plus flower shape. There are 15 divisions: 14 cover the garden hybrids and one the species and species hybrids. Knowing which division a variety is in will help you predict when it will flower and what its characteristics will be.

Single Early (division one) These are the earliest tulips to flower, typically in early to mid-spring; many can also be forced to flower even earlier under glass. The bulbs can then be lifted early, so are ideal for beds where summer bedding will follow.

'Keizerskroon' (page 36)
'Yokohama' (see page 38)
'Apricot Beauty' (page 40)
'Charles' (page 42)
'Generaal de Wet' (page 44)
'Prince Carnival' (page 46)
'Brilliant Star' (page 48)
'Bellona' (page 50)
'Flair', *see above* (page 52)

Double Early (division two) Large, full blooms up to 10cm (4in) across make these tulips impressive, but some varieties are prone to flopping over unless grown in a sheltered site. They start to flower in early spring, albeit a little later than Single Early tulips; some flower from early to mid-spring.

'Willemsoord' (page 56)
'Monte Carlo' (page 58)
'Peach Blossom', *see above* (page 60)
'Schoonoord' (page 62)
'Electra' (page 64)

Triumph (division three) These are mid-season tulips, coming into flower from mid- to late spring. The large blooms on sturdy stems make them ideal for border planting or for growing as cut flowers.

'Barcelona' (page 68)
'White Dream' (page 70)
'Princess Victoria', *see above* (page 72)

Darwin Hybrids (division four) Tall with large flowers, these mid-season tulips flower in mid- to late spring.

'Burning Heart' (page 76)
'Olympic Flame', *see above* (page 78)

Single Late (division five) These tall tulips have large flowers that are produced in late spring. There is a wide range of different colours within this group.

'Blushing Lady' (page 82)
'Halcro' (page 84)
'Sweet Harmony' (page 86)
'Menton', *see above* (page 88)
'Queen of Night' (page 90)
'Maureen' (page 92)
'Pink Diamond' (page 94)

 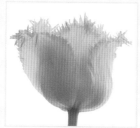 

Lily-flowered (division six) Pointed, reflexed petals give these flowers an elegant shape. Most are late-spring tulips, a few are mid-spring but all are invaluable in the garden.

'White Triumphator' (page 98)
'Jacqueline' (page 100)
'Ballade', *see above* (page 102)
'Elegans Alba' (page 104)
'Elegant Lady' (page 106)
'Queen of Sheba' (page 108)

Fringed (division seven) The petals of these late-spring tulips have an impressive fringed edge, making them very showy.

'Fancy Frills' (page 112)
'Blue Heron' (page 114)
'Burgundy Lace' (page 116)
'Hamilton', *see above* (page 118)
'Maja' (page 120)

Viridiflora (division eight) An unusual group, with a green stripe or flame on the back of the petals. They bloom in late spring.

'Artist' (page 124)
'Spring Green' (page 128)
'Esperanto', *see above* (page 130)
'Greenland' (page 132)

Rembrandt (division nine) The blooms painted by the Dutch Old Masters. A virus has caused the petals to be streaked with colour. Plant health regulations mean they are now not grown in the Netherlands and so are not commercially available.

Parrot (division ten)
Fringed, twisted petals give the appearance of a parrot's plumage. Depending on the variety the stems may or may not be sturdy, but in general they require a sheltered site. They flower towards the end of spring.

'Black Parrot' (page 136)
'Texas Gold', *see above* (page 138)
'Orange Favourite' (page 140)
'Flaming Parrot' (page 142)
'Fantasy' (page 144)
'Yellow Parrot' (page 146)
'Blue Parrot' (page 148)
'Estella Rijnveld' (page 152)
'Red Parrot' (page 154)

Double Late (division eleven) These have large double flowers, a bit like peonies. They flower towards the end of spring and need a sheltered spot as rain can flatten them. In the right place they have a long flowering season.

'Mount Tacoma' (page 158)
'Carnaval de Nice', *see above* (page 160)
'Bonanza' (page 162)
'Uncle Tom' (page 164)

Kaufmanniana (division twelve) Small tulips that flower in very early spring, these often have blooms that are bi-coloured. Some also have very attractive mottled foliage. They are ideal tulips for planting in containers, in the front of the border or for rockeries.

'Heart's Delight', *see above* (page 192)

Fosteriana (division thirteen) These can be used like Kaufmannianas and Greigiis, but are taller with large flowers, so could also be grown in flower beds. They flower from early to mid-spring.

'Candela' (page 168)
'Juan' (page 172)
'Orange Emperor' (page 174)
'Princeps', *see above* (page 176)
'Purissima' (page 178)

Greigii (division fourteen) The maroon mottling on the foliage is a feature of these tulips, which flower in early to mid-spring. Again, they are ideal for containers, the front of the border or rockeries.

'Cape Cod' (page 182)
'Plaisir' (page 184)
'Oratorio', *see above* (page 186)
'Yellow Dawn' (page 188)
'Toronto' (page 190)

Species (division fifteen) These have not been crossed or bred but occur naturally or have been selected from natural stock. Most are low growing with star-shaped flowers, and can be left to seed and naturalize in rockeries or grass.

'Lilac Wonder' (page 196)
'Tubergen's Gem' (page 198)
'Fusilier' (page 200)
'Whittallii', *see above* (page 202)

Single

Early

These are among the first tulips to flower, typically in early to mid-spring; many varieties such as 'Apricot Beauty' and 'Brilliant Star' are suitable for forcing under glass so they flower even earlier. On a cautionary note, earliness increases the chance of blooms being at the mercy of wind and rain. The simple flower shape and short sturdy stems will help them stand up to the weather, as does growing them in containers so you can move them into more sheltered positions.

Single Early **'Keizerskroon'**

FLOWERING PERIOD
Early spring
FLOWERING HEIGHT
35cm (14in)
INTRODUCED
1750

Two hundred and fifty years and still growing strong, this is one of the oldest tulip cultivars, yet it was awarded a coveted AGM award from the RHS as recently as 1993. 'Keizerskroon' (which means 'Emperor's Crown') is red with a broad yellow edge. Although fairly tall compared to the Kaufmanniana and Greigii hybrids, it can be grown in containers: choose deep ones such as wooden half-barrels. It combines well with wallflowers, creating a simple yet reliable cottage-garden style planting.

Single Early 'Yokohama'

This golden-yellow tulip is especially renowned for its long-lasting blooms, a useful characteristic for both a garden plant and a cut flower, as tulip flowers are generally rather fleeting. Note also the elongated petals with their pointed tips, a shape that makes for an elegant and refined bloom. 'Yokohama' is named after the Japanese city of the same name. This variety is suitable for forcing.

FLOWERING PERIOD
Early spring
FLOWERING HEIGHT
35cm (14in)
BREEDER
J.F. van den Berg & Sons
INTRODUCED
1961

Single Early **'Apricot Beauty'**

The delicate yet breathtaking colour of this early season tulip changes as the flower ages: as it opens up, the inside is revealed to be richer than the outside. There are few pastel shades in early spring, so this offers a real alternative to the usual run of brighter colours. Plant up several pots and position them on the patio, where you can enjoy their blooms and wavy leaves – it combines well with white tulips like 'Diana' or 'White Hawk'. 'Apricot Beauty' can be forced indoors as you would prepared hyacinths, flowering in late winter.

FLOWERING PERIOD
Early spring

FLOWERING HEIGHT
45cm (18in)

BREEDER
C. Vlugt van Kimmenade

INTRODUCED
1953

Single Early 'Charles'

Early tulips are valued for their wide range of flower colour in early spring, but keep in mind that they will peak when the weather may be wet and windy. To improve the chances of enjoying a prolonged display, opt for robust varieties with sturdy stems, like 'Charles', and plant in a sheltered spot. 'Charles' has eye-catching bright red flowers. Once open, they reveal a yellow base inside.

FLOWERING PERIOD
Early spring

FLOWERING HEIGHT
40cm (16in)

BREEDER
C.P. Alkemade Junior

INTRODUCED
1954

Single Early *'Generaal de Wet'*

This tulip was introduced a couple of years after the end of the Anglo-Boer War (1899–1902) and was named after farmer-turned-war-hero Generaal Christiaan Rudolph de Wet. Not many cultivars scoop an RHS Award of Merit in the year they are introduced; fewer still are going strong 100 years later. Its unique colouring – yellow-orange with delicate orange-red stippling – plus its very sweet scent make it still worth growing today. Plant outdoors for early colour in beds and borders, or indoors as a forced tulip.

FLOWERING PERIOD
Early spring
FLOWERING HEIGHT
40cm (16in)
INTRODUCED
1904

Single Early **'Prince Carnival'**

Like 'Generaal de Wet' (see page 45), this tulip is a sport of the old cultivar 'Prince of Austria', and shares the same sweet scent and warm-coloured blooms. The flowers are red and yellow flamed. Although 'Prince Carnival' (or 'Prins Carnaval') is a good garden variety, it can be hard to obtain, so keep in mind a modern alternative called 'Mickey Mouse', registered in 1960 by E. Kooi. It is similar in colour, but is a bit shorter at 35cm (14in) and has smaller flowers.

FLOWERING PERIOD
Early spring

FLOWERING HEIGHT
40cm (16in)

INTRODUCED
1930

Single Early **'Brilliant Star'**

'Brilliant Star' is also known by the Dutch as 'Christmas Tulip' because it can be forced into flower at this time. A historical tulip, whose raiser is unknown, it is still available and is especially popular in Scandinavia as it performs well in poor light. It is also used by breeders to pass on its fiery red colour to other taller-stemmed tulips. There are two sports to look out for: 'Joffre' (1931), yellow with red markings and only 13cm (5in) tall, and 'Sint Maarten' (1983), deep orange with red flames and 30cm (12in) tall.

FLOWERING PERIOD
Early spring
FLOWERING HEIGHT
30cm (12in)
INTRODUCED
1906

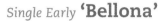

Single Early *'Bellona'*

The sweet scent of this tulip marks it out as something special. To best appreciate its fragrance and to protect the blooms from bad weather, grow a batch indoors, forcing them as you would prepared hyacinths. Alternatively, plant outside in the usual way choosing a warm sheltered position. These golden-yellow flowers would look stunning underplanted with a carpet of blue or purple violas or pansies. 'Bellona' is a sport from an orange-red tulip called 'Prince of Austria' that dates back to 1860.

FLOWERING PERIOD
Early spring

FLOWERING HEIGHT
50cm (20in)

BREEDER
H. de Graaf & Sons

INTRODUCED
1944

Single Early **'Flair'**

A fiery little tulip whose warm hues bring welcome colour in early to mid-spring. On close inspection, you will see that each flower is red and yellow with irregular stripes and flames. Once the flowers open, the yellow anthers stand out against the black at the base of the petals. 'Flair' is ideal for growing in pots because its stems are fairly short. To make the most of its colour, try using steel-grey aluminium planters or ceramic pots with a dark blue or black glaze.

FLOWERING PERIOD
Early spring

FLOWERING HEIGHT
35cm (14in)

BREEDER
Jac van den Berg

INTRODUCED
1978

Double

Early

These are impressive tulips with large blooms up to 10cm (4in) across. They start flowering in the early spring, albeit a little later than Single Earlies, so need protection from wind and rain. Those with short, sturdy stems are ideal for growing in pots and windowboxes. 'Monte Carlo' is fairly weather-resistant and has a lovely fragrance. 'Murillo' (1860) is an important historic Double Early that has produced more

sports than any other tulip. These, such as 'Electra', 'Schoonoord' and 'Willemsoord', can be grown together in a rainbow mixture as they have similar heights and flowering times.

Double Early **'Willemsoord'**

This tulip is a sport of 'Murillo', the most important historical Double Early tulip. 'Murillo' was introduced in 1860 by Gerard Leembruggen and it has produced 140 named sports, around 20 of which are still available. Amazingly, these were all natural mutations. 'Willemsoord' has a sport, 'Jan W. van Reisen', which is named after the person who discovered it in 1960. It is purple rather than carmine, but retains the striking white edge.

FLOWERING PERIOD
Early spring

FLOWERING HEIGHT
25cm (10in)

BREEDER
Paul Roozen

INTRODUCED
1930

Double Early 'Monte Carlo'

This money-spinning tulip occupies the largest hectarage in Holland. Commercial growers force millions of bulbs every year to produce cut flowers. 'Monte Carlo' is excellent in the garden, as confirmed by its AGM from the RHS. Plant in a raised bed or in pots and tubs to create splashes of spring cheer, or force a batch as you would prepared hyacinths and enjoy their fragrance indoors. There is one sport called 'Monsella' (1981), which is yellow with a red flame; the markings are variable – even on 'Monte Carlo' there is sometimes the merest hint of red.

FLOWERING PERIOD
Early spring

FLOWERING HEIGHT
30cm (12in)

BREEDER
Anton Nijssen & Sons

INTRODUCED
1955

Double Early **'Peach Blossom'**

'Peach Blossom' was one of the first sports of the important historical tulip 'Murillo' (see 'Willemsoord', page 57) and, with its deep rose-pink peony-like flowers, is remains the most popular. Borne on short stems, the flowers are ideal for small pots or perhaps even windowboxes, particularly if they are underplanted with golden-leafed feverfew (*Tanacetum parthenium* 'Aureum'). Since its introduction, 'Peach Blossom' has produced several sports – 'Garanza', 'Robert Spencer' and 'Willem van Oranje'.

FLOWERING PERIOD
Early spring

FLOWERING HEIGHT
25cm (10in)

INTRODUCED
1890

Double Early **'Schoonoord'**

A sport of 'Murillo' (see 'Willemsoord', page 57), its discoverer and date of discovery are unknown, although it won an award in 1909. Its white colour means that 'Schoonoord' will mix beautifully with any of the other 'Murillo' sports, while its short stems also make it a neat candidate for pots and windowboxes: try it in combination with blue grape hyacinths (*Muscari*) for a cool, refreshing planting.

FLOWERING PERIOD
Early spring
FLOWERING HEIGHT
25cm (10in)

Double Early 'Electra'

It is easy to mistake this lovely tulip for a peony, yet it is much more versatile. With its short, sturdy stems, it can be grown in containers, either outdoors or forced under cover, or it can be used in a mixture of bedding tulips of 'Murillo' sports. For an eye-catching spring bedding scheme, combine it with the white 'Schoonoord' (see page 62); if you cannot obtain 'Electra', use its sport 'Willemsoord' instead (see page 57).

FLOWERING PERIOD
Early spring

FLOWERING HEIGHT
25cm (10in)

INTRODUCED
1905

Triu

This popular and varied group arose by crossing
Single Early with Single Late tulips, to produce
offspring that flowers from mid- to late spring.
They make good cut flowers and are easy to force,
so are the most important group for commercial
growers in the Netherlands. Simple blooms on
sturdy stems make them ideal for spring bedding,
and they have a wide range of colours and flower
shapes. Pale purple 'Atilla' was a popular choice
for bedding but as the stock gets weaker, consider 'Barcelona',
a more recent variety that is a bit pinker and taller.

mph

Triumph **'Barcelona'**

This is one of the most outstanding of the newer Triumph tulips thanks to its intense colour and strong stems. The blooms start off egg-shaped rather than the conical shape normally associated with Triumph tulips, and then open out as they mature. 'Barcelona' is very similar to the well-known 'Attila', a popular tulip since its introduction in 1945, the main difference being that 'Barcelona' is slightly pinker and a bit taller. As the stocks of 'Attila' start to weaken and become less vigorous, 'Barcelona' is in line to replace it.

FLOWERING PERIOD
Mid-spring

FLOWERING HEIGHT
60cm (24in)

BREEDER
Hybris

INTRODUCED
1989

Triumph **'White Dream'**

The Triumph group was developed from the early twentieth century onwards to meet the demand for tulips for the popular bedding displays in parks. Such tulips needed to be uniform, like soldiers on parade, with little variation in height or flowering time and with sturdy stems so that there would be no slouching in the ranks. 'White Dream' has charming flowers, although they are smaller than is typical for a Triumph tulip, and it is a reliable choice for beds or large tubs.

FLOWERING PERIOD
Mid-spring

FLOWERING HEIGHT
50cm (20in)

BREEDER
J.F. van den Berg & Sons

INTRODUCED
1972

Triumph **'Princess Victoria'**

White and carmine almost blend together
to produce the soft, feminine coloration
in this flower. As is typical of the (relatively)
more recent Triumph tulips, 'Princess
Victoria' has a sturdy habit and is a good
forcing tulip. 'Los Angeles' – apricot-red
flowers with a yellow edge – is another
variety with blended colours introduced
by the same breeder.

FLOWERING PERIOD
Mid-to late spring

FLOWERING HEIGHT
50cm (20in)

BREEDER
J.F. van den Berg & Sons

INTRODUCED
1979

Darwin

Hybrids

These tulips produce big, bright blooms on tall stems in mid- to late spring. A fairly new group, the Darwin Hybrids were introduced by Dirk Lefeber who crossed Darwin tulips with *Tulipa fosteriana*, the resulting hybrids being more vigorous and less prone to viruses than the original ones. 'Apeldoorn' is a well-known example: it is easy for suppliers to produce because it divides easily and has produced many sports – usually red and/or yellow. There are some variations of red, yellow and orange, such as 'Burning Heart', an ivory bloom with a pink-red flame.

Darwin Hybrids **'Burning Heart'**

A gorgeous colour combination, this has an ivory-cream flower with a delicate flame of pink-red. Peer inside an open bloom and you will see that the flame markings are brighter still. 'Burning Heart' is a recent sport of 'Ivory Floradale', an ivory-cream tulip with small amounts of red spotting; this in turn is a sport of a red tulip called 'Floradale'. Like most Darwin Hybrids, 'Burning Heart' has large flowers on strong, sturdy stems that make it a most lovely cut flower.

FLOWERING PERIOD
Mid-spring

FLOWERING HEIGHT
55cm (22in)

BREEDER
J.N.M van Eeden

INTRODUCED
1991

Darwin Hybrids **'Olympic Flame'**

Aptly named, this tulip looks like a flaming torch with red markings on yellow petals. This is both an excellent garden variety and cut flower, as it has both sturdy stems and scented flowers. Although this particular tulip was introduced by A. Verschoor, it is a sport of Dirk Lefeber's 'Favourite', whose work, crossing the Fosterianas with the Darwin tulips, was largely responsible for creating the Darwin Hybrids in the first place. These include a couple of other tulips, 'Oxford' and 'Parade', that are similar to 'Olympic Flame' but taller.

FLOWERING PERIOD
Mid-spring

FLOWERING HEIGHT
55cm (22in)

BREEDER
A. Verschoor Jr

INTRODUCED
1971

Single

Late

This is a large diverse group that contains
tulips previously classified as Darwin tulips
and Cottage tulips. Both were derived from
Florist tulips, which were selected for their
colour and their ability to 'break' – to show
streaks of colour. Single Lates tend to be tall
and within this group is 'Maureen', one of the
tallest with large white flowers. Their height
makes them ideal spring bedding but their late flowering means
there might be a delay in following on with summer bedding.
There is a wide range of colours within this group, including the
deservedly popular, almost black, 'Queen of Night'.

Single Late **'Blushing Lady'**

This is one of the newest in a long line of Single Lates bred by D.W. Lefeber & Co. First a Lily-flowered tulip, 'Mariette', was crossed with a Greigii resulting in the salmon-pink-red 'Temple of Beauty' (1959). 'Temple of Beauty' produced many sports including 'Blushing Beauty' (1983), with soft orange flowers with red flames and a yellow centre. 'Blushing Beauty' produced an intensely coloured sport in 'Blushing Lady' which, like 'Temple of Beauty', has tall stems and long-lasting, elongated flowers.

FLOWERING PERIOD
Late spring

FLOWERING HEIGHT
75cm (30in)

BREEDER
D.W. Lefeber & Co
and J.N.M.
van Eeden

INTRODUCED
1991

Single Late *'Halcro'*

A very tall tulip that is also one of the
last to come into flower, its long-lasting
blooms can still be showing colour into
early summer in Holland, if the weather
is not too warm. Plant the bulbs in drifts
in the middle or towards the back of a
herbaceous border, and wait for their
striking egg-shaped, carmine-red blooms
to add structure and vibrant colour to
the emerging green foliage. With such
long-lasting blooms, 'Halcro' also makes
a reliable cut flower.

FLOWERING PERIOD
Late spring

FLOWERING HEIGHT
70cm (28in)

BREEDER
Segers Bros

INTRODUCED
1949

Single Late **'Sweet Harmony'**

Dutch growers have a nickname for this tulip – eggnog with cream (*advocaat met slagroom*) – which describes its lovely colour very well. Although now quite an old tulip, it is still popular for the combination of pale yellow with an ivory-white edge. 'Sweet Harmony' would look wonderful alongside the other Single Late tulip 'Blue Aimable', with its lavender-mauve flowers. The strong stems, shorter than most Single Late tulips, make this a useful tulip for planting in tubs.

FLOWERING PERIOD
Late spring

FLOWERING HEIGHT
45–50cm (18–20in)

BREEDER
Jac B. Roozen

INTRODUCED
1944

Single Late **'Menton'**

This is tall and sturdy with a very big egg-shaped flower. It has deep pink petals with an orange flush and is one of several sports produced by 'Renown', a rose-red tulip with large flowers that, in turn, originated as a seedling from 'Mrs John T. Scheepers'. Menton is a city on the French Riviera renowned for its gardens and flower displays. Here citrus trees, palms and mimosa thrive in the sunny, subtropical climate, and so too does the heat-tolerant tulip named after it. Likewise, it is a suitable for the warmer southern states of the USA.

FLOWERING PERIOD
Late spring
FLOWERING HEIGHT
65cm (26in)
BREEDER
W. Dekker & Sons
INTRODUCED
1971

Single Late 'Queen of Night'

An outstanding tulip and the nearest
we have to a black, it is very special yet
easy and reliable. Try planting a group
in front of silver-leafed perennials, pair it
with the perennial wallflower *Erysimum*
'Bowles' Mauve' or team it with white,
pink or red Single Late tulips. A recent
sport is the double-flowered 'Black Hero',
registered by J. Beerepoot in 1984: stocks
are only just becoming available, but it
sounds exciting.

FLOWERING PERIOD
Late spring
FLOWERING HEIGHT
60cm (24in)
BREEDER
J.J. Grullemans & Sons
INTRODUCED
1944

Single Late 'Maureen'

This is one of the tallest tulips with long, strong stems and egg-shaped, white blooms. It is a seedling of 'Mrs John T. Scheepers' – another Single Late tulip. Tolerant of warm conditions it is popular in the southern states of the USA. Commercial growers in the south of France grow it as a cut flower for Paris markets, because they can get it to bloom a fortnight earlier than their rivals in Holland. The AGM from the RHS will reassure gardeners that 'Maureen' has plenty to offer as a garden variety, although it is expensive compared to most tulips.

FLOWERING PERIOD
Late spring

FLOWERING HEIGHT
70cm (28in)

BREEDER
Segers Bros

INTRODUCED
1950

Single Late **'Pink Diamond'**

When this clear but soft pink colour
was first introduced it was so much in
demand by the Japanese that bulbs were
very expensive. Now, although it is still
popular in Japan, prices are on a par with
other special tulips and it costs no more
than, say, 'Queen of Night' (see page 90).
Study the flowers close up and you can
see that the edges of the outside petals
are a lighter pink. Once the blooms open,
a grey-yellow centre can be seen. When
using this tulip in colour schemes, try
to combine it with white, cream or pale
blue flowers.

FLOWERING PERIOD
Late spring
FLOWERING HEIGHT
50cm (20in)
BREEDER
C.N. Verbruggen
INTRODUCED
1976

Lily-flo

wered

The characteristic of this group is the pointed and reflexed petals that give these flowers their elegant shape. Typically, the young flowers have a tight vase-shape, then they open out into star-like blooms. It is well-worth growing a row or two for cut flowers. Lily-flowered tulips were originally bred from old Darwin and Cottage tulips; only since 1958 have they had their own group. Most are tall and flower in late spring. There are plenty of colours to choose from, from the rich coloured 'Queen of Sheba', red-edged with gold, to the simple elegance of 'White Triumphator'.

Lily-flowered **'White Triumphator'**

Introduced in 1942, this tulip still triumphed over its rivals to receive the coveted AGM from the Royal Horticultural Society in 1995 – and so has proved to be appropriately named! It has sturdy stems bearing long-lasting, beautifully-shaped blooms. And, as white looks good with any colour, you cannot go wrong by this popular tulip. Plant drifts of it in the middle or at the back of a border packed with lush green foliage, or adopt a more formal approach and use it as a spring bedding plant with other late-flowering tulips or with a low underplanting.

FLOWERING PERIOD
Late spring

FLOWERING HEIGHT
60cm (24in)

BREEDER
C.G. van Tubergen

INTRODUCED
1942

Lily-flowered **'Jacqueline'**

Like all Lily-flowered tulips, 'Jacqueline' offers both elegant flower shape and robust weather resistance. The deep pink flowers look lovely underplanted with white or pink double daisies or combined with a white Lily-flowered tulip. 'Jacqueline' was bred by Segers Bros; although better known for their work on the Fringed tulips, they turned their attentions to the Lily-flowered types and this was one of the last they registered. It is tall but has very strong stems that provide good wind tolerance, making it an excellent garden tulip.

FLOWERING PERIOD
Late spring

FLOWERING HEIGHT
70cm (28in)

BREEDER
Segers Bros

INTRODUCED
1958

Lily-flowered **'Ballade'**

The flowers of this variety are special, with a broad white edge. Plant in dappled shade or where it is sunny only part of the day, to protect the white edge from sun scorch. As the petals are wider and less reflexed than most Lily-flowered tulips, blooms are more goblet-shaped. Ballade also flowers earlier than others in this group and is one of the few Lily-flowered types suitable for forcing as cut flowers. Several sports are in the pipeline: 'Ballade Dream' ('Sonnet'), purple-red with a yellow base; and 'Ballade Orange' ('Je T'aime'), orange with a yellow margin.

FLOWERING PERIOD
Mid-spring
FLOWERING HEIGHT
55cm (22in)
BREEDER
Nieuwenhuis Bros
INTRODUCED
1953

Lily-flowered '**Elegans Alba**'

A unique colour combination in a tulip, there is simply no other variety like this one, with its lily-flowered petals of purest ivory edged with a very narrow red rim. This historical tulip won an Award of Merit in 1895 but details of the raiser and the circumstances of its discovery are unknown. Stocks are slow to bulk up and difficult to source, so if you obtain any bulbs, you should treasure them. As a garden plant, the stems can be a little weak so it is well worth finding a sheltered site to plant this variety in. With such delicate colouring it is best to keep nearby planting subtle; violas make excellent companion plants.

FLOWERING PERIOD
Late spring

FLOWERING HEIGHT
50cm (20in)

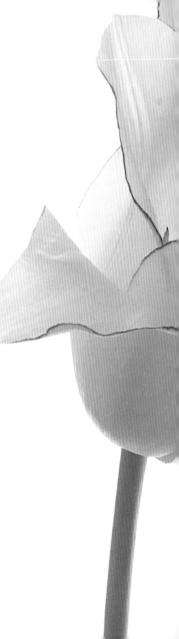

Lily-flowered **'Elegant Lady'**

Creamy yellow overlaid with a warm pink flush, this tulip has truly exquisite colouring so make sure you grow it in a spot where you can linger and appreciate it. 'Elegant Lady' was registered by Niewenhuis Bros of Lisse, a nursery that, from the 1930s to the 1960s, was a prominent breeder of many excellent Lily-flowered tulips including 'Ballade', 'Queen of Sheba', 'West Point' and 'Maytime'. Flowering in late spring, 'Elegant Lady' often escapes the worst of the weather. The pointed and reflexed petals make a graceful silhouette that then opens out in warm weather.

FLOWERING PERIOD
Late spring

FLOWERING HEIGHT
60cm (24in)

BREEDER
Nieuwenhuis Bros

INTRODUCED
1953

Lily-flowered **'Queen of Sheba'**

This truly majestic tulip is prized for its
glowing colour and refined lily-flowered
shape. The slenderness of the young
flower is emphasized by the narrowest
golden-yellow edge, and as the flower
matures it opens wide to reveal an
unexpected greenish centre. This makes
an excellent garden plant from the
practical point of view too, as it has
long-lasting blooms on strong stems.
So all in all, no wonder it is still winning
awards nearly fifty years after it was
first bred during the Second World War.

FLOWERING PERIOD
Late spring

FLOWERING HEIGHT
60cm (24in)

BREEDER
Dr W.E. de Mol and
A.H. Nieuwenhuis

INTRODUCED
1944

Fring

ed

This group takes its name from masses of short needles at the edges of the blooms. This edging means the flowers loose their simple outline, but are showy and fascinating at close quarters. Like them or not, the tulips in this recently created group (1981), previously grouped as Single Lates, are hard to ignore. They make excellent cut flowers or alternatively an eye-catching container subject, but few are suitable for forcing. Most Fringed tulips arose as sports between 1925 to 1930 but some were bred by Segers Bros who undertook a lot of hybridizing in the 1960s and 1970s.

Fringed **'Fancy Frills'**

'Fancy Frills' is one of the earliest Fringed tulips to come into flower, ideal for a patio planter, and one of the very few in this group that is suitable for forcing. It shows the characteristic serrations on the edges of the petals, plus it has an attractive rose-pink flower with a white base. Segers Bros closed in 1975, only three years after this lovely tulip was released, and the stock was transferred to a W.A.M. Pennings.

FLOWERING PERIOD
Late spring

FLOWERING HEIGHT
45cm (18in)

BREEDER
Segers Bros

INTRODUCED
1972

Fringed *'Blue Heron'*

The colour of this tulip is unique and when the flower opens, a paler inside is revealed that subtly contrasts with the darker outside. Add to this the short, crystalline fringe and you have a truly special flower. Grow it where you can appreciate the blooms almost at eye level, or cut to enjoy indoors. 'Blue Heron' is one of the cultivars from Segers Bros, who specialized in breeding Fringed tulips.

FLOWERING PERIOD
Late spring

FLOWERING HEIGHT
60cm (24in)

BREEDER
Serger Bros

INTRODUCED
1970

Fringed *'Burgundy Lace'*

One of the last of the Fringed tulips to flower, this is a useful insurance if you live in an area with cold springs. The tall stems bear carmine-red blooms, making it an ideal companion for the yellow-flowered 'Maja' (see page 120), which has a similar habit and flowering time. Introduced in 1961, 'Burgundy Lace' was one of the early crosses made by Segers Bros; the uniform colour was much in demand in the 1970s and 1980s, and it is still popular today as it is a good perennial tulip.

FLOWERING PERIOD
Late spring
FLOWERING HEIGHT
70cm (28in)
BREEDER
Segers Bros
INTRODUCED
1961

Fringed **'Hamilton'**

This tall, elegant tulip was one of the last to be registered by Segers Bros. Deep yellow flowers exhibit the crisp fringe along the edge of the petals, characteristic of the Fringed group. Its flowers are particularly long lasting and are worth placing where you can look at them at close quarters and marvel at the delicate serration. At one time 'Hamilton' was used commercially as a forcing tulip, but it fell from favour as it was susceptible to a virus; however, the present stock is clean so it makes a good garden plant.

FLOWERING PERIOD
Late spring

FLOWERING HEIGHT
65cm (26in)

BREEDER
Segers Bros

INTRODUCED
1974

Fringed **'Maja'**

This close-up of 'Maja' shows the intricacy of the serration that makes Fringed tulips so fascinating. They are a subtle version of Parrot tulips, which also arose originally as natural sports. Rather than leave the emergence of new Fringed tulips to chance, in the 1960s and 1970s breeders took matters into their own hands. 'Maja' is one of the results. It has late-flowering primrose-coloured blooms, which are a particularly attractive shade of yellow and the plants are very sturdy growers.

FLOWERING PERIOD
Late spring
FLOWERING HEIGHT
65cm (26in)
BREEDER
Segers Bros
INTRODUCED
1968

Viridi

This group of tulips with green markings on the backs of the mature blooms takes its name from the Latin *viridi* meaning 'green' and *flora* meaning flower. Flowers with a green tinge have a certain cachet, particularly among flower arrangers, but many are good garden plants too, as they are long-flowering starting in late spring. There are records of tulips with green markings dating back to at least 1700 but most of the varieties available today were introduced in the 1950s to 1960s. The most popular is 'Spring Green' with its white flowers with a green flame.

flora

Viridiflora **'Artist'**

A dwarf Viridiflora, with salmon petals flamed with green, this makes a good garden tulip, particularly in containers. 'Artist' was the result of a cross between the orange 'Generaal de Wet' (see page 45) and the Single Late red 'Mayflower'. As with many intricately marked tulips, enthusiasts became obsessive about them, and for a spell in the 1950s there was a mini-tulipomania for some new cultivars of 'Artist'. One example was 'Hollywood', a bright red-and-green tulip, which sold for £500 per kilogram. Other sports of 'Artist' are 'Golden Artist', with golden-orange petals and a green flame, and more recently 'Green River', which has variegated leaves of dark green and pale yellow.

FLOWERING PERIOD
Late spring

FLOWERING HEIGHT
30cm (12in)

BREEDER
Captein Brothers

INTRODUCED
1947

Viridiflora **'Spring Green'**

For discerning gardeners, including the late Christopher Lloyd of the Great Dixter garden in Sussex, this is the very best Viridiflora. The cool combination of the green flame and white edge seems contemporary and it is easy to imagine it arising out of bold foliage plants like hostas and ferns, yet 'Spring Green' was actually introduced in the psychedelic 1960s. As one of the taller Viridifloras, it can be used in the middle and at the back of the border or in beds with an underplanting. If you can spare any, try cutting the flowers to enjoy them indoors.

FLOWERING PERIOD
Late spring

FLOWERING HEIGHT
50cm (20in)

BREEDER
P. Liefting

INTRODUCED
1969

Viridiflora **'Esperanto'**

This tulip has the same dwarf habit as
'Artist' but its flowers are red with green
markings. The silver-white variegated
leaves make it an interesting subject for
growing in containers; an underplanting
of white violas would echo its colouring.
'Esperanto' is a sport of 'Hollywood',
which in turn is a sport of 'Artist' (see
page 124).

FLOWERING PERIOD
Late spring

FLOWERING HEIGHT
30cm (12in)

BREEDER
J. Pranger

INTRODUCED
1968

Viridiflora **'Greenland'**

The appeal of this tulip is that the green
appears as an elegant flame running up
the middle of the petals rather than
covering the whole bloom, which would be
no fun at all. These tulips were only given
their own group in 1987, before which
they were classified by flowering time.
'Greenland' (or, more correctly, 'Groenland')
has a strong stem and is the largest of
the group. It has produced a recent sport
called 'New Wave', that is a Parrot version
of the parent.

FLOWERING PERIOD
Late spring

FLOWERING HEIGHT
55cm (22in)

BREEDER
J.F. van den Berg & Sons

INTRODUCED
1955

Parr

ot

The fringed, twisted petals make these distinctive and there is sometimes extra feathering on the surface, too. Parrot tulips arise as sports of existing varieties so apart from their parrot appearance they are similar in colour, height and flowering time to the parent. Parrot tulips flower in late spring but even at this time of year a sheltered site is best as the blooms are prone to rain damage and in some varieties the stems are not sturdy enough to support the flowers.

Parrot **'Black Parrot'**

The black-maroon flower makes this a highly desirable Parrot tulip. Its stems are stiff enough to make it a successful spring bedding plant and it would combine very well with yellow or orange wallflowers. When growing it as a container plant, choose a silver- or grey-coloured container. Plant where you can enjoy it at fairly close quarters. This tulip emerged as a sport of the Single Late tulip 'Philippe de Comines' (1891), with a small maroon-black flower.

FLOWERING PERIOD
Late spring

FLOWERING HEIGHT
50cm (20in)

BREEDER
C. Keur & Sons

INTRODUCED
1937

Parrot **'Texas Gold'**

'Texas Gold' is one of the latest-flowering tulips: fortunately it is able to withstand the higher temperatures that can occur in late spring. The yellow flowers initially have green markings, but in time they develop a very narrow red edge. As with some other Parrot tulips (see 'Orange Favourite', page 140), the stems do tend to curve, so try to position them where they can be viewed and appreciated from below. In 1958 J.J. de Wit found and registered a red-flamed sport of 'Texas Gold', which he named 'Texas Flame'.

FLOWERING PERIOD
Late spring

FLOWERING HEIGHT
45cm (18in)

BREEDER
G. van den Meij & Sons

INTRODUCED
1944

Parrot *'Orange Favourite'*

Here is one of the most fragrant tulips, yet there is plenty of visual interest as well, with the lovely orange flowers lightly streaked with green feathers. Like most Parrot tulips, it becomes more exciting as the blooms open and the symmetry gives way to a wild exotic look – in this particular variety, the petals open to show a prominent yellow centre. The stems can be rather lax, and the blooms can flop, so a container placed where you can look up at the open flowers is ideal.

FLOWERING PERIOD
Late spring

FLOWERING HEIGHT
50cm (20in)

BREEDER
K.C. Vooren

INTRODUCED
1930

Parrot 'Flaming Parrot'

In Japan, this particular variety, with its subtle coloration and beautiful form, is highly sought after for cut-flower arrangements. It has the appearance of an old Rembrandt tulip but the markings are due to a natural mutation rather than a virus. This extrovert Parrot tulip is a sport of 'Red Parrot' (see page 154); the only difference between the two is the colour. In all other respects – such as sturdy stems and flowering time – they are the same.

FLOWERING PERIOD
Late spring

FLOWERING HEIGHT
70cm (28in)

BREEDER
P. Heemskerk

INTRODUCED
1968

Parrot **'Fantasy'**

This is one of the oldest Parrot tulips,
but is still very popular and a favourite
with flower arrangers. Compared to
modern Parrot tulips, the stems are
rather weak, so it needs a sheltered
position to achieve an upright display.
Alternatively, grow it in a large hanging
basket so that when the flowers droop
down you can look up to admire them.
'Fantasy' arose as a sport of 'Clara
Butt', a salmon-pink tulip, at one time
a very popular cultivar of the Darwin
group. This group has since been
consolidated into the Single Late group.

FLOWERING PERIOD
Late spring

FLOWERING HEIGHT
55cm (22in)

INTRODUCED
1910

Parrot **'Yellow Parrot'**

Here we see a Parrot tulip opened out to full extent, with its ruffle-edged petals almost waving like flags in the wind. In contrast, when the flower first emerges it looks quite sedate, and this change in form as the bloom matures goes some way to explaining why gardeners and flower arrangers alike find the Parrots so fascinating. 'Yellow Parrot' was introduced in 1973, so it is relatively new. Like many of the more recent Parrots, it has strong stems that support the full blooms well, making it a good garden variety – hence its Dutch Trial Garden Award.

FLOWERING PERIOD
Late spring

FLOWERING HEIGHT
55cm (22in)

BREEDER
C. van Dijk

INTRODUCED
1973

Parrot 'Blue Parrot'

The only violet Parrot tulip now in commercial cultivation, this was found as a mutation in a stock of 'Bleu Aimable', a Single Late tulip. It was registered by J.F. Charles Dix, who was legendary for his work on many tulip groups and also for his longevity – he died aged 106. Its large flowers are supported well by stiff, upright stems, making it very gardenworthy. As the flowers open, ruffled petals curve outwards to reveal a dark centre against the pale stigma.

FLOWERING PERIOD
Late spring

FLOWERING HEIGHT
55cm (22in)

BREEDER
J.F. Charles Dix

INTRODUCED
1935

Parrot **'Estella Rinjveld'**

The blooms of this variety are like
generous scoops of raspberry ripple ice-
cream. Its alternative name, 'Gay Presto',
sums up its exuberance well. With its
characteristic feathered plumage, 'Estella
Rijnveld' arose as a mutation of 'Cordell
Hull', a Single Late tulip with red flowers
and white flames. Tulip aficionados
value 'Estella Rijnveld' for her plentiful
feathers. The stems are shorter than
typical Parrot tulips, which makes for a
sturdy plant, ideal for containers or an
open border.

FLOWERING PERIOD
Late spring
FLOWERING HEIGHT
50cm (20in)
BREEDER
Segers Bros
INTRODUCED
1954

Parrot *'Red Parrot'*

Parrot tulips are some of the showiest and there is always great demand for them. As a result, they are rather expensive and supplies can be limited. But even a handful, with their large fringed and ruffled blooms, will pack a punch. Strong colours abound and 'Red Parrot', with its very intense red coloration, is a perfect example. Flower arrangers adore Parrot tulips – apart from the pollen that stains – but they are excellent garden plants too. 'Red Parrot' has long, strong stems that can withstand bad weather if planted in a sheltered site.

FLOWERING PERIOD
Late spring

FLOWERING HEIGHT
70cm (28in)

BREEDER
J.C. Evers

INTRODUCED
1940

Double

The large double flowers bear a resemblence to peonies hence their other name: 'peony-flowered tulips'. These are amongst the last tulips to flower so they should miss the worst of cold. They do best when sheltered from rain which can fill the bloom and topple them. If the weather is kind, they are long flowering and once planted the bulbs are long-lived, too, so they are a good choice for sheltered borders or long-term bedding. Colours range from the simple white of 'Mount Tacoma' to the rich deep red of 'Uncle Tom' to the vibrant red and white 'Carnaval de Nice'.

Late

Double Late 'Mount Tacoma'

Large bulbs of 'Mount Tacoma' produce white flowers with attractive markings on the petals, setting this variety apart from other white double tulips. Smaller bulbs are less likely to produce the markings. Grow in a sheltered site: a border backed with shrubs to act as a windbreak is ideal. An alternative is to grow it to use as a cut flower. This is an old variety but it is still popular as it can be used to create cool, calming plantings of white and green. Try it with an underplanting of white-and-green variegated hostas and maybe some white double daisies (*Bellis perennis*).

FLOWERING PERIOD
Late spring

FLOWERING HEIGHT
45cm (18in)

BREEDER
Polman-Mooy

INTRODUCED
Before 1924

Double Late *'Carnaval de Nice'*

Eye-catching and fully double, this is just what you need to announce the arrival of spring. It is a sport of 'Nizza' that mutated in two ways: the flower colour changed from red and yellow to red and white, and the foliage sported to produce silver-edged leaves. A similar tulip, 'Gerbrand Kieft', was introduced by Hybrida in 1951, named after one of its founders. Kieft did much to preserve Double Late varieties when they were out of favour, so it is apt that his namesake is one that has survived.

FLOWERING PERIOD
Late spring

FLOWERING HEIGHT
50cm (20in)

BREEDER
C.G. van Tubergen

INTRODUCED
1953

Double Late **'Bonanza'**

As its name suggests, this tulip delivers something extra: really full double blooms that flower for a long period by tulip standards. Fortunately, the heavy flowers are well supported by strong stems, a characteristic that makes it a good choice for forcing. The warm colours of orange-red with a yellow edge ensure this is a welcome spring flower. If you cannot find supplies, a suitable substitute is 'Allegretto', another Double Late tulip whose flowers are also red with a yellow edge, but it is slightly shorter at 35cm (14in).

FLOWERING PERIOD
Late spring

FLOWERING HEIGHT
40cm (16in)

INTRODUCED
1943

Double Late **'Uncle Tom'**

This cultivar is the deepest red of the Double Late tulips and is currently enjoying a revival, as garden designers encourage us to be bolder with colour schemes. Like all peony-flowered varieties, a spell of dry weather is required while they are flowering, otherwise the stems may not be able to support the blooms. Alternatively, you could grow them in rows as cut flowers and pick them as they are opening. For the same shape of flower in an unusual silver-pink, go for the more widely available 'Angélique'.

FLOWERING PERIOD
Late spring

FLOWERING HEIGHT
45cm (18in)

BREEDER
Zocher & Co.

INTRODUCED
around 1935–1939

Foster

iana

These tulips are derived from *Tulipa fosterianna*, a species tulip from Tajikistan and Uzbekistan that arrived in the Netherlands in 1906. The species has large, glossy red blooms with a black blotch, edged with yellow at the base and was a parent of the Darwin Hybrids. Characteristics of this group are bright blooms, broad, often maroon-flecked foliage and long-lived bulbs that can come back year after year. They flower from early spring and compared to the Geigii and Kaufmanniana tulips they are taller with larger flowers so they could be used for spring bedding.

Fosteriana **'Candela'**

'Candela' is an good example of the plant breeder's magic. By crossing the scarlet *Tulipa fosteriana* with Single Early tulips, breeders created varieties that had the shape and flowering time of the species but with an increased colour range. 'Candela' is a prime example; its oblong flowers are buttercup-yellow, yet they appear slightly later than the Single Early tulips. Once open, the flowers reveal their black anthers – a sharp contrast with the yellow. You can rely on this variety to emerge year after year, so it is a good choice for a low-maintenance border.

FLOWERING PERIOD
Mid-spring
FLOWERING HEIGHT
35cm (14in)
BREEDER
K. van Egmond & Sons
INTRODUCED
1961

Fosteriana **'Juan'**

Dutch growers were attracted by the vivid red colour and long flowers of the species *Tulipa fosteriana*, and it proved to be a good breeding plant. Many hybrids were introduced from the 1940s to the 1970s, including 'Juan'. The eye-catching combination of deep orange blooms with prominent yellow bases is unique; put this together with the maroon stripes on the foliage and you have a tulip that is colourful enough to be grown in a bed on its own.

FLOWERING PERIOD
Early spring

FLOWERING HEIGHT
45cm (18in)

BREEDER
C.G. van Tubergen

INTRODUCED
1961

Fosteriana 'Orange Emperor'

This tulip was obtained by crossing the vivid 'Red Emperor' with a now-extinct orange Single Early tulip called 'Fred Moore'. The result is a softer colour with a yellow centre that is much easier to place in the garden than the original 'Red Emperor'. On close inspection of the young flowers, you will sometimes see green feathering along the midrib; although subtle, such markings are desirable features in any tulip and add to its value as a cut flower.

FLOWERING PERIOD
Mid-spring

FLOWERING HEIGHT
40cm (16in)

BREEDER
K. van Egmond & Sons

INTRODUCED
1962

Fosteriana **'Princeps'**

One of the easiest ways to grow tulips, particularly if your soil is wet and sticky, is to plant them in containers. This sturdy tulip, with its short stems topped with red flowers, is perfect for small pots and windowboxes. 'Princeps' is a clone that was selected by Jan Roes from a batch of *Tulipa fosteriana* bulbs imported from Central Asia, and is of particular interest to breeders as it retains the resistance to tulip-breaking virus.

FLOWERING PERIOD
Early spring

FLOWERING HEIGHT
25cm (10in)

BREEDER
Jan Roes

Fosteriana **'Purissima'**

The only white-flowered member of the
Fosteriana group, 'Purissima' (sometimes
sold as 'White Emperor') is adored for its
large, bowl-shaped blooms, that are ably
supported against any adverse weather
by sturdy grey-green stems and foliage.
The yellow at the base of the petals is a
hint that it might produce yellow sports,
as it did with 'Yellow Purissima' (1980)
and more recently 'Purissima King'
(1994), which is red with a yellow base.

FLOWERING PERIOD
Early spring
FLOWERING HEIGHT
45cm (18in)
BREEDER
C.G. van Tubergen
INTRODUCED
1943

Greig

& Kaufmanniana

ii

The species *Tulipa greigii* was introduced from Central Asia in the 1870s. Its distinctive features are its short stems and foliage. The leaves are low-growing, crinkle-edged and with maroon markings. Hybrids arising from this species are ideal for early spring colour. *Tulipa kaufmanniana* is known as the waterlily tulip because the flowers open flat and wide in the sun. It is one of the earliest into flower and also easy to grow. There are many hybrids that share those attributes, and any that also have Greigii parentage have mottled maroon foliage.

Greigii **'Cape Cod'**

Named after Cape Cod, near Boston, this particular Greigii tulip is popular in the USA. Like the other Greigii tulips bred by Hybrida in the 1950s, it has attractive mottled foliage and a neat habit, so is excellent for providing pockets of early colour in small spaces. What makes this one different from its red-flowered relatives is its colour; from a distance, the flowers give the impression of an apricot-coloured haze, but close-up you can see that they have red outer petals with yellow edges, while inside they are yellow with a feathered red stripe.

FLOWERING PERIOD
Early to mid-spring

FLOWERING HEIGHT
30cm (12in)

BREEDER
Hybrida

INTRODUCED
1955

Greigii **'Plaisir'**

Most Greigii hybrids are gardenworthy, but Plaisir is one of the best. It is ideal for small gardens, windowboxes, patios and balconies. When the flowers first appear they have an elegant pointed shape; as they mature, you notice the feathered markings and the contrast of the dark centre. Its sport, 'Californian Sun', yellow with a large scarlet flame and registered by J. Prins & Sons in 1988, makes an interesting variation.

FLOWERING PERIOD
Early to mid-spring

FLOWERING HEIGHT
25cm (10in)

BREEDER
Hybrida

INTRODUCED
1953

Greigii **'Oratorio'**

You will notice this little tulip as soon as its beautiful mottled leaves come through the soil. Later it will reward you with rosy-red blooms. This is one of a number of Greigii cultivars bred by the growers' co-operative Hybrida in the early 1950s; another is the more familiar scarlet 'Red Riding Hood'. However, many find the colour of 'Oratorio' easier to place and a little more special. Its low habit makes it ideal for raised beds, rockeries, small pots and windowboxes.

FLOWERING PERIOD
Early to mid-spring

FLOWERING HEIGHT
30cm (12in)

BREEDER
Hybrida

INTRODUCED
1953

Greigii **'Yellow Dawn'**

These flowers, with their sunrise colours, are stunning and as they age they open out like stars. 'Yellow Dawn' also possesses many practical attributes: it has a stocky habit and its sturdy growth makes it an easy subject for rockeries, containers and windy gardens. To bring spring interest to a border or rose garden, plant these tulips towards the front to enable their maroon-mottled foliage to frame the edge. The flowers come back reliably year after year, making them an invaluable addition for low-maintenance planting schemes.

FLOWERING PERIOD
Early to mid-spring
FLOWERING HEIGHT
35cm (14in)
BREEDER
Hybrida
INTRODUCED
1953

Greigii **'Toronto'**

These warm coloured blooms nestling in their lightly speckled foliage offer easy and reliable colour. 'Toronto' is a typical Greigii tulip but with the bonus that it is sometimes multiflowered, which means it can produce more than one flower per stem. Tuck these bulbs into the smallest of spaces and you will be sure of a big impact. The flowers reveal yellow at the base of the petals, overlaid with bronze. This hint of other colours has resulted in two interesting multiflowered sports: 'Orange Toronto' (1987) – a marigold-orange colour – and 'Quebec' (1991) – scarlet with green margins on its petals and a yellow base.

FLOWERING PERIOD
Early to mid-spring

FLOWERING HEIGHT
35cm (14in)

BREEDER
Jac Uittenbogaard & Sons

INTRODUCED
1963

Kaufmanniana **'Heart's Delight'**

The short stems of the Kaufmannianas are not suitable for the lucrative cut-flower market, so little breeding work has been done on them in the past 40 years or so. This hybrid was bred in the early 1950s. Hybrids like 'Heart's Delight', which have some Greigii parentage, also have attractive maroon stripes or mottling on their leaves and the waterlily-shaped flower is shared by others in its group.

FLOWERING PERIOD
Very early spring

FLOWERING HEIGHT
20cm (8in)

BREEDER
C.G. van Tubergen

INTRODUCED
1952

Speci

es

Within this group are naturally occurring species tulips, that is those that for the most part have not been bred or crossed. Most are low-growing with small, star-shaped flowers and can be left to self-seed in rockeries or grass. Those with particular garden appeal include: 'Lilac Wonder', a little tulip for a hot dry spot; 'Tubergen's Gem', a selection of a species, for hot, dry spots; 'Fusilier', a selection of *Tulipa praestans* with up to six flowers per stem and very easy to grow; and 'Whittallii', small bronze-yellow flowers that start cup-shaped and then open out into small stars.

Species **'Lilac Wonder'**

No wonder this little tulip is a best seller: Anyone who sees the intense lilac and egg-yolk yellow combination on the small, star-like flowers and the waxy shine of its leaves will be enticed into buying. 'Lilac Wonder' is a cultivar of the smaller, less showy *Tulipa bakeri*, although it resembles another species, *T. saxatilis*, which has led to some confusion over its full name. UK taxonomists refer to it as *T. saxatilis* Bakeri Group 'Lilac Wonder' and it is often sold as *T. saxatilis* 'Lilac Wonder' – however, the Dutch registration committee believes it is closer genetically to *T. bakeri*. To be sure of plenty of flowers, plant it in a warm, dry spot, perhaps in a rockery or at the foot of a sun-baked wall. If you have any gaps between paving slabs, these could be a perfect site as it spreads a little via stolons (spreading stems with roots).

FLOWERING PERIOD
Late spring

FLOWERING HEIGHT
15cm (6in)

BREEDER
Kees Visser

INTRODUCTED
1971

Species 'Tubergen's Gem'

What a delight to watch the change in
colour as these graceful blooms unfurl.
At first the flowers are red with just the
hint of a yellow edge; then, as their petals
partly open, the yellow inside is revealed.
The species (*Tulipa clusiana* var. *chysantha*)
can be shy to flower, but 'Tubergen's Gem'
is larger and this increased size means
that it has bigger bulbs with more
reserves, increasing the reliability of
flowering. Even so, this is a small tulip,
so plant it where it will not be smothered
by neighbouring plants. A warm, dry
place like a rockery would suit it best.

FLOWERING PERIOD
Early to mid-spring

FLOWERING HEIGHT
25cm (10in)

BREEDER
C.G. van Tubergen

INTRODUCED
1969

Species **'Fusilier'**

This cultivar selected by Jac Roozen has so much to offer: 'Fusilier' has up to six flowers per stem and the blooms are an almost unbelievably bright colour. It also has incredible flowering impact in very small spaces – you could easily tuck a row of 'Fusilier' in the front of a narrow or packed bed. It is very easy to grow as well. While many of the smaller species bulbs are rather tricky, this one has larger, tougher bulbs and once planted it will be long lived. For an even more colourful effect, you could plant the sport, *Tulipa praestans* 'Unicum', which has a pale yellow rim around each leaf.

FLOWERING PERIOD
Early spring
FLOWERING HEIGHT
35cm (14in)
BREEDER
Jac B. Roozen

Species **'Whittalli'**

This tulip is named after Ernest Whittall, a British man who lived in Turkey and who discovered this species while plant hunting in his spare time. *Tulipa whittallii* has bright bronze flowers touched with yellow. The blooms are cup-shaped at first and then they open out into a star. Large bulbs may yield two flowers per stem. Markings sometimes vary; there may be a green tinge to the outside of the flower and yellow-margined black basal marks inside, and the leaves may have red-purple margins.

FLOWERING PERIOD
Mid-spring

FLOWERING HEIGHT
30cm (12in)

BREEDER
Collected by Ernest
Whittall, Turkey

INTRODUCED
1929

Tulips

Tulips are easy to grow if you follow three basic principles: always buy top-quality bulbs, choose the right position for them and plant them correctly. With care, almost all tulips will flower for many years. In cold or exposed gardens, concentrate on mid- to late-season tulips and in warm climates, put the emphasis on early flowerers. You could even plant an early and a late tulip in the same planting hole or plant several layers of bulbs. Finally, remember that the colourful foliage that some varieties have will extend the period of interest.

in the garden

Tulips as annuals

Tulips grown as spring bedding plants in municipal parks are a familiar sight. Typically, circular or rectangular beds are cut out of lawn and planted in a pattern using one or more tulip varieties and a carpet of a lower-growing plant. You may want to adapt the idea for your garden by using spring bedding on a small scale but where it will have a big impact on your day-to-day life. You could, for example, plant tulip bedding alongside the path to your front door or at the foot of a window. Small beds that are regularly viewed from indoors – such as those that are visible while you are washing up – are ideal for spring bedding schemes.

Perfect partners

When it comes to choosing partners for your tulips there are lots of possibilities. You can have great fun scanning bulb and seed catalogues and making plans for your plantings. One classic pairing is a froth of pale blue forget-me-nots punctuated with red tulips; for a more restful variation try yellow, pink or white tulips, or plant some pink- or white-flowered forget-me-nots with a pink or white tulip.

Wallflowers offer warm hues of reds, yellows and oranges. Most are at their peak in late spring, so late-season tulips like 'Queen of Night' or Lily-flowered types work best. For the greatest impact, you will need a single-colour wallflower rather than a mixture, so it is worth growing your own from seed the previous summer.

For a lower-growing partner to your tulips, there are plenty of options among the different-coloured polyanthus and pansies. To accompany yellow tulips, a red polyanthus with a golden eye would be pleasing, whereas deep pink tulips generally look better with pure white or pink. A drift of purple or blue pansies or violas would look great with any colour of tulip and white tulips help to make a small gardens look bigger. Pick up on the maroon-mottled or striped foliage of the Greigii hybrids by teaming them with red double daisies (*Bellis perennis*) or a dark red pansy.

At renowned gardener Christopher Lloyd's garden at Great Dixter in Sussex, where there are many ideas for innovative plant combinations, tulips are paired with lupins. The emerging lupin foliage acts as a foil for the tulips, and when the tulip flowers are over, the lupins follow on. The lupins are pulled up and discarded after flowering and the bulbs harvested and stored when dormant.

right: The Lily-flowered 'West Point' stands to attention in front of blue grape hyacinths providing plenty of impact and contrast.

Tulips in containers

Tulips have the widest colour range of any of the spring bulbs, which makes them ideal for containers where they can be grown as single subjects or as part of a mixed planting.

Container growing also relieves you of having to prepare and plant in difficult soils such as heavy clay, and allows you to move pockets of spring colour to where they will have most impact. Pots of Double Early varieties like 'Peach Blossom' or 'Willemsoord' can be given shelter in a cool conservatory, then taken outside when the weather is favourable. When the display is over, the containers can be whisked away. For a succession of spring colour on a patio, start with a container of Kaufmanniana or Greigii hybrids; when these are over, replace with a pot containing any early or mid-season tulip, and when that is past its best, bring on a tub of Lily-flowered or Parrot varieties.

Choose a large enough container and any tulip can be grown successfully, but if you are planting up smaller pots (those that are under 30cm/12in diameter) or windowboxes in exposed locations it is best if you stick to the shorter varieties, under 35cm/14in high – look among the Kaufmanniana, Fosteriana and Greigii types for candidates. Also, keep in mind the multiflowered types like 'Toronto' and *Tulipa praestans* 'Fusilier', which are perfect for growing in small containers. Good single subjects for larger pots near seats include tulips with unusual shapes or markings that are best appreciated close up: these include the Fringed, Parrot or Viridiflora types.

Ideas from spring bedding schemes can be scaled down to be used in containers: tulips with an underplanting of dwarf wallflowers, double daisies, polyanthus, violas or grape hyacinths (*Muscari*), with flowers like tiny bunches of grapes, are easy ones to start with.

left: Varieties of different heights but with the same flowering time can be planted in layers.

Tulips as perennials

In countries with hardy zones 3–8 (such as the UK, most of northern Europe and parts of the USA) tulips can be treated as perennials if they are planted deeply enough. However, in warmer climates with hardy zones 9–10 (such as the southern states of the USA) only some species, like *Tulipa bakeri* 'Lilac Wonder', are suitable for this treatment. (Here, it can even be difficult to grow tulips as annuals and the bulbs will usually need a cold treatment – store in a refrigerator in a paper bag – for 8–10 weeks prior to planting. They will need to be planted deep and topped with a mulch to keep them cool.) Bulb catalogues from the relevant countries usually indicate those tulips that are good as perennials.

Treating tulips as perennials saves a lot of work. Take this one stage further and underplant with low-growing perennials rather than traditional spring bedding. Raid the rockery or alpine section of the garden centre for possible candidates such as aubrieta, *Aurinia saxatilis* (formerly *Alyssum saxatile*) or *Iberis sempervirens.*

Another easy way to create a low-maintenance pairing is to grow tulips alongside dwarf shrubs – go for those with strong foliage colours and you will not have to worry about matching the flowering times. The best shrub for pairing with tulips must be a golden-leafed variety of the dwarf *Spiraea japonica*. Try 'Goldflame', which has orange tips to the young foliage in spring and makes a fiery scene with red or orange tulips. For a more subtle foil of blue-green, bright green or orange-brown, consider the wide range of dwarf hebes, while the yellow-green of the evergreen perennial *Euphorbia polychroma* reaches its peak in mid- to late spring, making it an ideal companion for mid- or late-season tulips in red, orange or purple.

Tulips will bring spring colour to bare ground near trees or large shrubs as long as the site receives sun for at least half the day. Deciduous trees and shrubs let more light through than evergreens so, for example, under an apple tree you could plant late-season pink or white tulips and a carpet ground cover like the silver-leafed deadnettle (*Lamium maculatum*). A bed with nothing but roses looks dull in spring, so brighten it up with an edging of dwarf tulips. Any of the smaller tulips would be suitable and they can be left in the ground year after year. Larger evergreens can be used as a foil for tulips; *Photinia* x *fraseri* 'Red Robin', for example, with its bright red new foliage, would make an exciting background for red or orange tulips.

right: Placing pink tulips near dark-leaved foliage creates a striking contrast.

Tulips in borders

Mid- to late spring in a herbaceous border sees shoots poking up above the ground and low mounds of green foliage forming over the bare earth. Add some tulips to this scene and from mid-spring onwards, the border will be alive with flowers and will appear to be more advanced.

The wide colour palette of tulips offers unlimited scope. You could ring the changes with a totally different effect to the summer scheme – bold red-and-white Parrot tulips such as 'Estella Rijnveld' preceding a summer border of pastels, for example. Alternatively, give a taste of the colours to come, planting a yellow tulip like the early flowering 'Candela' or the later-flowering 'Yellow Parrot' as a precursor to a blue-and-yellow summer border, for example. The Single, Double Early, Double Late, Triumph, Darwin Hybrids, Parrot and Lily-flowered groups are most suitable for the middle and back of borders, while smaller tulips such as the Greigii hybrids are ideal as edging.

For long-lived tulips, the foliage needs to be left to die down naturally so that it can feed the bulb ready for the following season. To disguise the unattractive fading bulb foliage, position the tulips in the middle or at the back of the border and at the front, accompany with plants that have camouflaging strap- or grass-like foliage, such as red hot pokers (*Kniphofia*) or the very lovely day lilies (*Hemerocallis*).

Layering bulbs

Several layers of different spring bulbs with a range of flowering times can be planted either in the ground, in a raised bed or in a large pot. The pot needs to be at least 25cm (10in) deep. This technique will extend the flowering season without taking up any more space. However, it can work out very expensive: approximately 150–200 bulbs will be needed for an area 1m (3ft) square.

Tulips in such schemes can be paired with another tulip (an early flowerer such as one of the Greigii or Kaufmannianas with a late-season tulip chosen from Single or Double Late, Lily-flowered or Parrot types), plus one or more of the earlier flowering smaller bulbs such as bulbous iris (*Iris reticulata*), crocus or dwarf daffodil. At the Keukenhof Garden in the Netherlands they plant crocus on top of early tulips on top of late tulips, which ensures a sequence of colour from early to late spring. To plan your scheme, choose four or five subjects on the basis of their flowering time, height and how deeply they need to be planted.

Winter pot plants

Growing prepared hyacinths is a good way of having flower colour indoors in winter. Some tulips can be planted in early autumn in the same way, although they need a longer cool period (12 weeks). Try the particularly early 'Brilliant Star', 'Apricot Beauty' or 'Bellona'. Use half a dozen bulbs per 15cm (6in) pot. Pot them up in compost with their necks just below the surface. Water and keep in a cool, dark place. Once rooted, the bulb will produce top growth; when you see 8cm (3in) of top growth bring indoors in a cool place, but keep in the dark. The increase in temperature will lengthen the stems; once over 10cm (4in), move to a cool, light place to encourage the top growth to turn green.

Unusual sites

A rockery, raised bed or alpine trough is the perfect home for the smaller species tulips. They may be shy to flower at first, but are very long lived. Spring bulbs naturalized in grass between trees or on a slope also make a wonderful easy-to-maintain feature. Tulips are rarely naturalized in this way as their foliage is so large, but some, such as *Tulipa kaufmanniana* and its hybrids, are worth a try. Over the years, they will spread to create a carpet. You will need an area of grass where the first cut can be delayed until after most of the bulb foliage has died back.

below: Wallflowers and tulips are a familiar and dependable pairing.

Tulip

There are literally thousands of tulip varieties to choose from, which is part of the attraction, but even the keenest gardener can only grow a selection in any one year. The tulips featured in this book come from a unique private collection in the Netherlands and they can be be relied on as being gardenworthy and among the best in their particular division. The essential guidelines to buying bulbs, planting, maintainance and aftercare, including avoiding pests and treating common diseases, are laid out very simply in the following pages.

Care

In autumn, you can buy packs of tulip bulbs in supermarkets and department stores, but for a greater range or if you want to choose your own loose bulbs – which makes them cheaper – you should visit a garden centre. For a specific variety or for large numbers of bulbs, buy from a specialist and be sure to order early.

Look for large, heavy bulbs, preferably 11cm (4½in) or 12cm (4¾in) – bigger bulbs give bigger flowers. The brown outer coating (the tunic) that protects the bulbs should be present and more or less intact. Reject dried-out or chalky-looking bulbs as well as any with drops of what looks like brown glue on them – this is a sign that they have been in contact with 'sour' rot. However, the superficial blue mould on the tunic is not a problem – simply rub the mould off and store the bulbs in a dry place until you plant them. If you buy packets of bulbs, open them as soon as you get home, and remove and destroy any infected bulbs. Store the bulbs spread out on a plastic or metal mesh tray in a cool, dry, dark place. (Note that handling tulip bulbs can bring some people out in an itchy rash, so if you have sensitive skin wear gloves. Tulip bulbs are listed as being poisonous if eaten so keep them out of reach of children.)

Trays of potted tulip plants for sale with buds just showing colour are a tempting sight in spring. The advantage is that they have come through the winter unscathed and are certain to flower. Also, in spring you can see exactly where you want pockets of colour. There is a catch, of course: you will pay over the odds for them, and the choice will be limited.

When and how to plant

Amost all spring-flowering bulbs should be planted in autumn, but tulips are an exception: they can be planted any time from mid-autumn to early winter. Late planting will still give impressive displays and the flowering will only lag by a week or two compared to bulbs planted earlier in the autumn. The ideal time is mid- to late autumn; any earlier and the emerging foliage in spring will be vulnerable to fungal disease and frost damage.

Tulips benefit from deep planting – a depth of 10cm (4in) is a minimum, 15cm (6in) is better. Deeper planting of 20–25cm (8–10in) means you can leave the bulbs in the ground and plant summer bedding on top. Sometimes it is not possible to plant deeply – if the topsoil is shallow for example, or you have hundreds of bulbs to plant and little time. In such circumstances shallow planting at 5–8cm (2–3in) will suffice if you only want to treat the tulips as annuals.

The right place

As long as the bulb does not rot in a waterlogged soil over winter, you are more or less guaranteed a tulip. That said, a position with light from all sides will produce straighter stems – important in the taller varieties – while blooms will be retained longer in a sheltered site.

If you want to keep your bulbs from one year to the next, planting in the right place is important. Tulips do best on a free-draining garden loam, in a spot that is warm and dry over the summer when the bulbs are dormant. If you have problems with waterlogging, you may improve drainage by digging in garden compost or grit but you will need large quantities, so consider growing tulips in raised beds of free-draining topsoil or in containers.

Beds and borders

Choose a sunny site in the border, the further back the better so that the emerging perennials will hide the dying tulip foliage in early summer. Scatter the bulbs randomly, either in groups of 20 or more for a cluster of colour or in a drift that snakes in and out of other plants.

Make a hole and place a bulb in it, pointed end uppermost. Replace the soil on top of the bulb and firm it down gently. To layer bulbs, use a spade to dig out an area 1m (3ft) square and 20cm (8in) deep, plant the first layer of bulbs, cover with soil, plant the next layer, and so on.

When planting a formal spring bedding scheme, mark out the area to be planted and set out all the bedding first, spacing it about 30cm (12in) apart – 15cm (6in) for the small types and dwarf varieties. Plant the bedding, then set out and plant the tulips, usually 15cm (6in) apart.

Rows

A straight line of tulips standing to attention looks striking in a formal garden, especially if you have a narrow bed alongside an evergreen hedge. Growing in rows also makes sense when tulips are grown for cutting. If you do opt to grow tulips as cut flowers, the Triumph and Darwin Hybrids are those used commercially, but consider more unusual or pricey subjects like the Parrot, Viridiflora or Lily-flowered tulips. Prevent the build-up of soil-borne diseases by incorporating tulips into a three-year crop rotation – they do well on ground that has grown potatoes the year before.

To plant a row of tulips, use a garden line to mark out a straight line. Dig a trench at least three times the height of the bulb and space out the bulbs evenly along the bottom, leaving 5–15cm (2–6in) between them, depending on variety. Cover the bulbs with soil and firm the ground with your foot. Finally, label the trench.

Aftercare

After planting, little aftercare is needed apart from watering if the soil is very dry, unless you have problems with mice,  squirrels, pests and diseases (see below), or if you want the bulbs to flower in future years. If this is the case and there has been a lot of heavy rain over the winter and you have a free-draining soil, apply a feed as growth gets underway. One low in nitrogen but rich in potash would be suitable – either a proprietary bulb fertilizer for use in spring or a tomato feed once a week after flowering until the leaves die down. If the soil is fairly fertile you can get away without feeding. Remove the faded flowers immediately after flowering to direct the plant's energy back down into the bulb.

When the foliage has died down, lift the bulbs, dry them and clean to remove any soil, then store in a well-ventilated place until you replant in mid- to late autumn. If the foliage has not yet died down and the tulips are in the way of the summer bedding, either replant in another part of the garden so the leaves can die down naturally or go straight on to drying and storing them.

Container plantings

Containers should be at least 30cm (12in) across and deep, although 20–25cm (8–10in) would do for species tulips. The tulips are normally planted more densely than in the ground, so are best discarded each year, in which case use your preferred potting mix. Place a generous layer of crocks over the drainage holes and add compost to a depth of 10cm (4in). Position the tulip bulbs, starting in the centre and working outwards; they can be very close but not touching. Cover with more potting compost so the tips of the bulbs are just showing. Now plant the underplanting (or another layer of bulbs), and this time fill in the spaces around the edge of the pot. Add more compost to 2.5–5cm (1–2in) below the rim, firm down and water well. Water regularly once the leaves start to grow. If you want to keep the bulbs for planting out in the garden next year, liquid feed when the leaves are growing strongly and again as the buds form.

Tulip problems

This list looks daunting, but you are unlikely to experience more than one of these problems in any one year.

Droppers Swollen, root-like structures that grow from the top of the bulb down into the soil. Eventually, a new bulb will form lower down and flower after a couple of years. Droppers occur if you plant bulbs too shallow or if the soil dries out.

Eelworm This causes stems to bend, leaves to split and petals to stay green. The bulbs were probably infested prior to planting or the eelworm was in the soil and entered through a small wound. When the plant dies, the eelworm will move on to other plants so dig up and burn any infested plants promptly. To prevent the problem, buy from a reputable supplier and reject any soft bulbs.

Greenfly (aphids) Stored bulbs can be infested and damage can continue once they are planted. Spray with insecticide.

Mice Bulbs in store or in the ground may be nibbled. Try a covering over the ground of wire netting (mesh size no more than 1cm/½in) or of prickly leaves like holly. Indoors, set traps.

Poor flowering In time, tulip bulbs form clumps of smaller bulbs around them known as offsets. If left, the tulips will decline or even not flower at all, so separate and remove some of the offsets when the bulbs are lifted.

Root and foot rot Caused by soil-borne fungi. The base of the stem decays and the rot spreads through the plant. Remove and destroy infected plants and ensure garden hygiene by removing decaying plant debris and always using a clean water source.

Slugs and snails These cause holes in leaves, stems, flowers or even bulbs. Growing bulbs in containers or raised beds helps reduce the risk. You may need to resort to slug pellets; follow the instructions on the packet to minimize the danger to wildlife. A suitable biological control is worth trying, but this can be expensive over a large area.

Squirrels In gardens where squirrels abound, protect bulbs over winter. A covering of chicken wire secured at the edges works well.

Tulip fire A form of botrytis (grey mould), the symptoms are a brown scorching of the young foliage, followed by sooty specks on the leaves and flowers. Remove and burn infected leaves immediately, and spray the remaining foliage with a suitable systemic fungicide.

Virus Tulip-breaking virus still occurs sporadically. The first you will see of it is a plain-coloured tulip breaking into white or yellow streaks. It is spread by aphids and is more prevalent among late-flowering varieties. There is little you can do to stop the virus spreading, except remove and destroy the plant – although you might want to keep it if you like the pattern!

Index

Suppliers & societies

Suppliers

UK

Jacques Amand
The Nurseries
145 Clamp Hill
Stanmore
Middlesex HA7 3JS
Tel: +44 (0) 20 8420 7110

Avon Bulbs
Burnt House Farm
Mid-Lambrook
South Petherton
Somerset TA13 5HE
Tel: +44 (0)1460 242177
www.avonbulbs.co.uk

Bloms Bulbs Ltd
Primrose Nurseries
Melchbourne
Beds MK44 1ZZ
Tel: +44 (0)1234 709099
www.blomsbulbs.com

Peter Nyssen Ltd
124 Flixton Rd
Urmston
Manchester M41 5BG
Tel: +44 (0)161 747 4000
E-mail: peternyssenltd
@btinternet.com
Minimum order 50.

USA

Brent and Becky's Bulbs
7463 Heath Trail
Gloucester VA 23061
Tel: +1 804 693 3966
www.brentandbeckysbulbs.com

Bloms Bulbs Inc
491-233 Glen Eagle Square
Glen Mills PA 19342
Tel: +1 866 7 TULIPS
www.blomsbulbs.com

McClure and Zimmerman
108 W. Winnebago St
PO Box 368
Friesland WI 53935–0368
Tel: +1 800 883 6998
www.mzbulb.com

John Scheepers Inc
23 Tulip Drive
Bantam CT 06750
Tel: +1 860 567 0838
www.johnscheepers.com

Van Bourgondien
PO Box 1000, Babylon
New York 11702
Tel: +1 800 622 9959
www.dutchbulbs.com

White Flower Farm
30 Irene St
Torrington CT 06790
Tel: +1 800 503 9624
www.whiteflowerfarm.com

NETHERLANDS

Bijzondere Bloembollen
Postbus 653
2100 AR Heemstede
Tel: +31 (0) 252 530 353

Bloembollen Kwekerij
De Boender 6
2204 AC Nordwijk
Tel: +31 (0) 252 372193

Tulip World BV
Grasweg 71
1031 HX Amsterdam
www.tulipworld.com
Modern-looking website
offering an on-line bulb store
and design and style ideas
for using tulips

Van Tubergen
Postbus 144
8250 AC Dronten
Tel: +31 (0) 321 385141
E-mail:
tuber@oranjebandzaden.nl

Walter Blom & Zoon BV
Hyacinthenlaan 2
2182 DE Hillegrom
Tel: +31 (0) 252 519444
www.blomsbulbs.com

GERMANY
Blumenzwiebel Import und
Grosshandel
Postfach 1270
D–27342 Rotenburg/Wümme
Tel: +49 (0) 42 6163818

Dipl Ing Gardenbau
Fasanenweg 23
D–21717 Fredenbeck
Tel: +49 (0) 41 491640

Pflanzenspezialitäten
Potsdamer Strasse 40
D–14163 Berlin
Tel: +49 (0) 0 80 26251

Samengrosshandlung
Berliner Strasse 88
D–14169 Berlin
Tel: +49 (0) 30 81 14304

FRANCE
Baumaux
BP 100
54062 Nancy Cedex
Tel: +33 (0) 383 158 686
www.graines-baumaux.fr

Bulbes d'Opale
384 Boerenweg Ouest
59285 Buysscheure
Tel: +33 (0) 328 430 467

Ellebore
La Chamotière
61360 St-Jouin-de-Blavou
Tel: +33 (0) 233 833 772

Schryve Jardin
1315 route du Stent'je
59270 Bailleul
Tel: +33 (0) 328 492 740

AUSTRALIA/ NEW ZEALAND
Van Eeden Tulips
Dept G, West Plains Rd, 4RD
Invercargill
New Zealand
Tel: +64 (0) 3 215 7836
E-mail:
vaneedentulips@xtra.co.nz

New Gippsland Seeds and Bulbs
PO Box 1
Silvan
Victoria 3795
Australia
Tel: +61 (0) 3 9737 9560

Societies

International Bulb Society
PO Box 92136
Pasadena, CA 91109–2136
USA

Wakefield and North of
England Tulip Society
70 Wrenthorpe Lane
West Yorkshire WF2 0PT
A society that keeps the florist
tulip legacy alive via its annual
journal, meetings and shows.

Show Gardens

Keukenhof
Stationweg 166A
2161 AM Lisse
Netherlands
www.keukenhof.nl

Cambridge University
Botanic Garden
Cory Lodge
Bateman St
Cambridge CB2 1JF
England
Tel: +44 (0) 1223 336265
National Collection of tulips

Roozengaarde
PO Box 1248
Mount Vernon, WA 98273
USA
Tel: +1 866 488 5477
www.tulips.com
Show garden and supplier
of fresh flowers and bulbs via
Washington Bulb Co Inc

Acknowledgements

Author's Acknowledgements

I would like to thank Cees Breed for his help in selecting the tulips featured in this book, for providing information on their origin and for patiently answering my queries.

My thanks also extend to Clay Perry whose photographs have captured the essence of each variety so perfectly.

My interest in tulips first arose while I was working for *Gardening which?* magazine. Here I was able to visit tulip trials and the gardens of keen tulip growers; I will always remember the dedication and enthusiasm of Wendy Akers and her daughter Sarah Wainwright for the English tulips. My thanks also extend to the staff at the Royal Horticultural Society Library at Vincent Square, London.

It has been a real pleasure to work with the staff at Quadrille, in particular Hilary Mandleberg, the Project Editor, for her support and encouragement from start to finish.

Photographer's Acknowledgements

The photographer would like to thank the following: Marylyn Abbott, West Green House, Hartley Wintney, Hampshire; the Directors of the Keukenhof Garden, Lisse, Holland; Stanley Killingback, South Woodford, London; Peter Lloyd, Highgate, London; Jim Sellick, Pashley Manor, East Sussex; Maureen Thompson, Long Melford, Suffolk.